Original title:
Olive Sparks Amid the Phoenix Fern

Copyright © 2025 Swan Charm

Author: Sebastian Sarapuu
ISBN HARDBACK: 978-1-80563-205-4
ISBN PAPERBACK: 978-1-80564-726-3

Glistening Mornings of Renewal

In dawn's embrace, the light awakes,
With whispers soft, the heart remakes.
Each droplet shines like silver thread,
As dreams take flight from night-bound bed.

The world unfolds in hues anew,
A canvas kissed by morning dew.
With every beam that breaks the night,
A promise told in pure delight.

The trees, they dance with joyful grace,
In every branch, a sacred space.
The flowers bloom, their colors bright,
A symphony of sheer delight.

The brook hums low a soothing tune,
Beneath the watchful, glowing moon.
In nature's arms, we find our peace,
A moment's pause, a sweet release.

So greet the dawn, let worries fade,
In light of morn, new paths are laid.
For every day, a chance to grow,
In glistening mornings, life will flow.

An Awakening in Emerald Shadows

In emerald woods, where whispers dwell,
A tale unfolds, a secret spell.
With every rustle, life ignites,
In shadows deep, the magic bites.

The ferns arise with gentle sighs,
As sunlight filters through the skies.
Each leaf, a note in nature's song,
An anthem sweet, where hearts belong.

The creatures dance in playful glee,
With every step, they sing their plea.
In harmony, their spirits soar,
In emerald shadows, forevermore.

The brook weaves tales of olden days,
Reflecting light in winding ways.
As time slips by, the moments gleam,
An awakening in twilight's dream.

So wander deep where shadows play,
Embrace the night, welcome the day.
For in the dark, the light resides,
In emerald shadows, hope abides.

Celestial Sprouts in Warm Embrace

Beneath the stars that softly gleam,
The earth reveals its hidden dream.
With every seed, a promise sown,
In cosmic depths, new life is grown.

The moonlight bathes the garden's grace,
In tender beams, the shadows trace.
Each sprout that reaches for the night,
Is woven with celestial light.

The whispers of the cosmos call,
In stillness low, we hear them all.
With hearts attuned, we breathe the night,
In every glance, pure wonder's sight.

The breeze, it carries tales untold,
Of ancient times and dreams of old.
As petals dance in midnight's hands,
In warm embrace, the magic stands.

So let the stars your spirit guide,
With every step, let love abide.
For in the night where dreams take flight,
Celestial sprouts ignite the light.

Ferns of Illumination

In twilight's glow, the ferns unveil,
A silent path where secrets sail.
With emerald arms that stretch and weave,
They hold the tales we dare believe.

Each frond a story, rich and bright,
In gentle waves, they dance with light.
The whispers soft, the echoes near,
In ferns of illumination, cheer.

The shadows flicker, fears subside,
In nature's weave, our hearts confide.
With every rustle, hope ascends,
As light and dark begin to blend.

The earth is rooted in deep embrace,
Where life's reflections find their place.
Under the moon's soft, watchful gaze,
The ferns of light invoke our praise.

So wander forth where magic lies,
In every rustle, the spirit flies.
For in the night, let your heart sway,
In ferns of illumination, stay.

The Enchanted Grove's Resurgence

In the heart of the forest, secrets sigh,
Whispers of magic beneath the sky.
Ancient trees stretch their limbs wide,
Guardians of dreams where wonders bide.

Moonlight dances on leaves of green,
Echoes of laughter, a timeless sheen.
Roots intertwine in a lover's embrace,
Nature's embrace, a sacred place.

Rivulets murmur with tales of old,
Stories of bravery, tales of bold.
Life rekindles as shadows soar,
In this grove, we find so much more.

Radiance in the Botanical Resilience

Petals unfurl in the morning light,
Colors ablaze, a dazzling sight.
Nature's resilience, a fervent plea,
To rise with grace, like a soaring tree.

Between the stems, a brave heart glows,
The pulse of the earth, as wild wind blows.
Emerald leaves whisper with pride,
Guardians of stories, they won't hide.

In every bloom, a promise appears,
Hope interwoven through laughter and tears.
Roots delve deep into the warm, rich mire,
A testament to what we aspire.

Where Ferns Embrace the Flame

In the glade where the ferns entwine,
Fiery colors subtly shine.
A dance of shadows, a flicker of light,
Embers arise from the velvet night.

Breath of the forest, a warm embrace,
Nature's heartbeat, a sacred space.
Ferns unfurl in the softest grace,
Witness to wonders time can't erase.

A symphony whispers beneath the trees,
Carried by sighs of the gentle breeze.
In this haven where magic dreams,
Hope ignites in the softest gleams.

Elysian Glimmers in the Underbrush

In the shadows where secrets lie,
Elysian glimmers catch the eye.
Softly woven amidst the green,
Magic dances, a tranquil scene.

Moss carpets the earth like a woven shawl,
Echoes of life in a sylvan hall.
Whispers of fairies, a timeless tune,
In the heart of the wood, under the moon.

Each rustle and rustle, a story anew,
Of dreams come alive in the morning dew.
In the underbrush where the wild things roam,
Nature's embrace, forever our home.

Rebirth of the Emerald Aura

In shadows deep, where whispers play,
A seed lies still, awaiting day.
With tender roots and dreams anew,
The emerald aura starts to brew.

From cracks in earth, a sprout will rise,
To greet the sun and kiss the skies.
Each leaf, a promise of the morn,
A dance of life, where hope is born.

The forest sings, a sacred choir,
As nature weaves its endless fire.
With every drop of rain that falls,
The heart of earth within us calls.

With emerald hues that blend and flow,
Each color tells of tales we know.
Rebirth is but a magic spell,
In whispers deep, all fear dispel.

So bask in light, let shadows wane,
In emerald dreams, we'll break the chain.
For in this realm where spirits soar,
The emerald aura will restore.

The Forest's Fiery Embrace

Through tangled roots and tangled dreams,
The forest hums with fiery themes.
Its leaves aflame with vibrant hues,
A tapestry of reds and blues.

A crackling warmth within the night,
As shadows dance, a flickering light.
Each flick of flame ignites the soul,
In fiery embrace, we become whole.

The whispered secrets of the trees,
Inhaled with every breath of breeze.
With every crackle, spirits call,
In nature's arms, we risk our fall.

With every twirl of leaf and fire,
Our hearts awaken to desire.
We find our place in this vast maze,
Caught in the forest's fiery gaze.

So gather near and feel the heat,
In nature's grip, where souls will meet.
Together in this dance of fate,
The forest's fire, we celebrate.

Sparkling Verdure under the Sun

In morning light, the verdure glows,
A symphony where life bestows.
Each blade of grass, each flower bright,
A canvas painted by the light.

With sunbeams kissing every leaf,
The world awakes, beyond belief.
In sparkling hues, the day unfolds,
A tale of dreams and life retold.

The whispers of the breezes play,
As nature sings its sweet ballet.
In every corner, beauty's spun,
A dance of joy in all that's done.

Each droplet glimmers, pure and clear,
A treasure held, forever near.
In verdant fields, we find our peace,
A shining heart that will not cease.

So breathe the air, embrace the day,
In sparkling light, let worries sway.
For in this verdure, hope will rise,
A promise bright beneath the skies.

The Resilient Glow of Growth

From barren soil, a flicker starts,
The resilient glow ignites our hearts.
With every struggle, every fight,
A testament to strength and light.

In darkest nights, we search for stars,
In silent battles, bear our scars.
Yet in the dawn, we rise anew,
With courage found in skies so blue.

The whispers of the trees remind,
Of roots that anchor, hopes that bind.
With every heartbeat, we believe,
In growth, in life, in strength to grieve.

So lift your gaze, embrace the climb,
For every step is worth the time.
In every bloom, a chance to sing,
The resilient glow that life can bring.

From ash to flame, from dust to dream,
In every tear, a brighter gleam.
Together let us share the light,
For in our growth, the world ignites.

Verdant Hope on Charred Soil

In ashes deep, where shadows lie,
A spark ignites, beneath the sky.
Green tendrils stretch, reaching wide,
From charred remains, they will not hide.

For every burn, a promise grows,
In whispered winds, the courage flows.
Life's tenacity, a fierce delight,
In fragile forms, rebirth takes flight.

A grove emerges, brave and bold,
As stories of survival unfold.
Each leaf a tale, of battle won,
A testament to the rising sun.

With tender roots, they push on through,
Against the odds, their strength anew.
In verdant hues, the heart will soar,
A world reborn, forevermore.

So linger here, and take your stand,
On this renewed and sacred land.
For hope resides in every green,
And love will flourish, unforeseen.

Luminescence of Nature's Heart

Amid the dark, a glimmer bright,
The heart of nature, pure and light.
Through tangled woods, in fragrant air,
A dance of life, beyond compare.

Each spark of life, where shadows creep,
In secret glens, where silence weeps.
A shimmer swells, in petals wide,
As moonlit dreams and whispers bide.

The stream's soft song, a lullaby,
A twinkling tale, beneath the sky.
In every rustle, secrets told,
Of wonders new and wonders old.

With every dawn, the world awakes,
The vibrant pulse, the stillness shakes.
A warmth that casts away the chill,
In nature's glow, the heart stands still.

So breathe it in, this sacred space,
In every leaf, the light we chase.
For in the heart of every tree,
A luminescence, wild and free.

Life Amidst the Charcoal Veil

In twilight's hush, where shadows loom,
A charcoal veil, a whispered gloom.
Yet from the dark, a voice profound,
In silence sings, the life around.

Resilience dwells in every nook,
As fragile blooms in corners look.
With petals soft, they defy the night,
And draw forth strength from fading light.

Where cinders fall, new dreams arise,
In muted shades, the spirit lies.
With every heartbeat, hope will swell,
In secret realms, where courage dwells.

A tapestry, both fierce and frail,
As history weaves its subtle tale.
From ash and ember, life will play,
In vibrant hues, to greet the day.

So linger near, and take your cue,
From nature's art, both old and new.
For in the charcoal, life remains,
In every gust, in every rain.

The Glow of Renewal

In twilight's grasp, where shadows part,
A fire stirs within the heart.
With soft embrace, the dawn unfolds,
A canvas bright, a tale retold.

Violet hues kiss morning dew,
As sunlight weaves a path anew.
The world awakens, soft and slow,
In every nook, the bright seeds sow.

With gentle hands, the earth will mend,
In each moment, a chance to blend.
A symphony, of vibrant grace,
In every crack, a warm embrace.

From every struggle, blooms will rise,
To touch the sun and kiss the skies.
A cycle vast, of loss and gain,
In vibrant colors, hope will reign.

So watch the day, as life renews,
In every shade, in every hue.
For in the glow of every dawn,
The spirit's light will carry on.

Luminescent Dreams in Nature's Heart

In twilight's grasp, the shadows dance,
Where whispers weave in mystic trance.
A soft glow shimmers, calls us near,
Nature's heart beats, pure and clear.

The brook sings sweet with silver light,
As moonbeams twirl in gentle flight.
Each leaf a lantern, softly bright,
Guiding dreams through the endless night.

In mossy beds, where secrets sleep,
The world unveils its magic deep.
With every sigh, the stars align,
Crafting tales on nature's spine.

Creatures twirl in vibrant hue,
Their spirits dance, both old and new.
Through timeless woods, our spirits roam,
In luminescent dreams, we find home.

So linger here, let moments flow,
As gentle breezes start to blow.
In nature's heart, our souls ignite,
With dreams of wonders, pure delight.

Fires of the Forest Floor

Amidst the ferns, a spark awakes,
A fiery dance, the earth it shakes.
With crackling leaves in vibrant hues,
The forest glows, igniting clues.

Beneath the boughs, the embers spark,
In quiet corners, life leaves a mark.
Each flicker tells of days gone past,
Whispers of history, shadows cast.

The creatures gather, tales to share,
Of flickering lights and autumn air.
In smoky spirals, stories rise,
As stars above begin to prize.

The gentle flames, they weave and swoon,
Beneath the watch of a silver moon.
Together, hearts in warmth entwined,
In fires of the forest, peace we find.

So let the embers softly burn,
For in their glow, the world can turn.
A gathering place for spirits free,
In fires of the forest, souls agree.

The Radiant Leaf's Song

In autumn's clutch, the leaves take flight,
A swirl of color, pure delight.
With every rustle, whispers soar,
The radiant leaf begins to roar.

Each hue a story, soft yet bold,
A tapestry of truths untold.
In gentle breezes, melodies play,
The songs of nature lead the way.

From bright marigold to deep pine green,
A dance of life, forever seen.
Within the branches, joy takes wing,
The radiant leaf, forever sings.

With vibrant notes and laughter free,
In every flutter, a symphony.
So join the chorus, feel the breeze,
In nature's arms, we find our ease.

Let shadows stretch and daylight wane,
For in the dusk, there is no pain.
With every leaf, a song so sweet,
The radiant leaf, our hearts shall greet.

A Symphony of Light in the Trees

In emerald depths, the sunbeams play,
A symphony of light, night and day.
Through rustling leaves, soft notes arise,
The forest sings beneath the skies.

Upon the boughs, where shadows sway,
The light composes its joyful ballet.
Each ray a string, a note, a song,
Binding the earth where hearts belong.

In the gentle hush, a serenade,
Of nature's magic, never fade.
Harmony flows in whispers deep,
In every pulse, the world will keep.

Awake the heart, let spirits soar,
For in this light, we seek for more.
With each bright gleam, our dreams take flight,
A symphony of hope and light.

So wander forth, beneath the trees,
Let melodies dance upon the breeze.
In nature's hands, we are set free,
In a symphony of light, we'll be.

Celestial Images Through Verdant Eyes

In silence whispers the night sky,
Where stars like jewels brightly lie.
Soft breezes tease through emerald leaves,
As dreams take flight, and magic weaves.

Moonbeams cast a silver glow,
While shadows dance, moving slow.
Through verdant eyes the cosmos gleams,
Awakening the heart's deep dreams.

Each constellation tells its tale,
Of wondrous journeys, ships that sail.
With every twinkle, legends awake,
Through nature's lens, a world they make.

The forest breathes with ancient sighs,
Embracing all the night-time cries.
In harmony, they sing their song,
In rhythm with the stars lifelong.

So let us wander, hand in hand,
Through secret paths in this enchanted land.
Where celestial images softly glow,
Through verdant eyes, our spirits flow.

Resilient Radiance of the Woodlands

Each branch and bough holds stories old,
In whispered tales, the forest unfolds.
Resilient roots grasp the earth tight,
Embracing shadows, welcoming light.

Amidst the flowers, colors burst,
In every petal, nature's thirst.
The wind carries scents of the past,
In timeless beauty, enchantment cast.

Sunlight dapples the forest floor,
While creatures scurry, a life to explore.
In harmony, they weave through dusk,
An orchestra of life, vibrant and husk.

With every season, a cycle turns,
A lesson taught, a wisdom learns.
Resilient radiance in every tree,
A testament to life's tenacity.

Let us walk where the wild things roam,
In the heart of the woodlands, find our home.
For in nature's embrace, we truly thrive,
Resilient spirits, forever alive.

The Twilight's Luminous Embrace

As day bids farewell to the sun's bright rays,
The twilight emerges in delicate ways.
Colors blend in a soft tender kiss,
The world holds its breath for a moment of bliss.

Stars shyly peek from their covers of night,
In the tranquil hues, everything feels right.
Whispers of dreams dance on the breeze,
In twilight's embrace, the heart finds ease.

Moonlight spills on the path we tread,
Guiding our footsteps, where shadows spread.
A glimmering promise in the fading glow,
The night's gentle magic begins to flow.

While the sky dons a cloak of deep blue,
The secrets of twilight beckon anew.
In this space, our stories intertwine,
In luminous silence, forever we shine.

So let us cherish this quiet delight,
The twilight's embrace, the stars so bright.
For in these moments of stillness and grace,
We find our place in the vastness of space.

Glinting Sprinklings of Growth

In gardens lush where wildflowers bloom,
Each petal holds a story, dispelling gloom.
With every droplet that kisses the ground,
New life awakens, beauty unbound.

From inching sprouts to towering trees,
The earth envelops, swaying in the breeze.
In glinting sprinklings of morning dew,
The world is refreshed, as if born anew.

Every seed carries hope in its shell,
A whisper of nature, a magical spell.
In vibrant colors, the earth will sing,
Of changes that flourish with the arrival of spring.

From roots to blossoms, the cycle goes on,
A tapestry woven till dusk greets dawn.
Through patient growth, we learn to embrace,
The essence of life in this wondrous space.

So let us nurture, uphold, and tend,
To the glinting sprinklings that nature sends.
For in each moment of growth we find,
The beauty of life, intertwined and kind.

Aflame with the Essence of Renewal

In twilight's glow, the fire starts,
A whisper soft in muted hearts.
Old dreams are shed like autumn leaves,
A new dawn breaks, but who believes?

From ashes rise the cries of time,
Each flicker sings a hopeful rhyme.
With every spark, a tale reborn,
Resilience blooms, strong and adorned.

The shadows dance in amber light,
As nature weaves the day with night.
In every flame, a promise glows,
In every heart, the spirit flows.

Around the flames, the stories meld,
In stories told, our truths upheld.
Aflame with joy, our spirits soar,
With each new dawn, we seek for more.

Together we walk this path anew,
With hearts afire, our purpose true.
For in this dance, we find our way,
Aflame with life, the dawn of day.

The Fern's Dance with Fire

In secret glades where shadows play,
The ferns sway gently, come what may.
Their fronds embrace the flame's warm kiss,
A dance of life, a subtle bliss.

Through sunlit beams, they twist and twirl,
In golden light, their layers unfurl.
Fire flickers, amber and bright,
Nature's ballet in the fading light.

The smoke weaves tales of journeys past,
Whispers of wisdom from shadows cast.
In every ember, a story spun,
The fern and fire, two worlds as one.

With every leap, with every spin,
The fern invites the warmth within.
Through trials faced, the spirit thrives,
As dance and flame ignite our lives.

So let us join this sacred waltz,
With courage bright, we break down walls.
In fern's embrace, we'll learn to fly,
Together, we touch the starlit sky.

Luminescence in the Canopied Echoes

Beneath the boughs, where shadows dwell,
Luminescent whispers weave their spell.
Echoes of dreams from ages past,
In nature's grip, our hearts hold fast.

Each glimmer speaks of tales untold,
In ancient woods, where spirits bold.
The silver light through leaves cascades,
A dance of time, where life invades.

In the hush of night, a secret gleam,
Guides wanderers through the tangled dream.
Canopied whispers stir the nights,
With every flicker, the soul ignites.

Transcending night, we claim the dawn,
In luminescence, we are reborn.
Each step we take, the forest sighs,
A harmony of truth that never lies.

So heed the whispers, soft and light,
In echoed paths that lead to flight.
With every star, a wish takes wing,
In canopied echoes, our spirits sing.

Verdant Flames in the Twilight

As twilight drapes the world in peace,
A verdant heart begins to cease.
The fire warms with velvet grace,
A dance of light in a hidden place.

Leaves of emerald flicker bright,
Bathing all in warm delight.
Through whispered winds, the flames arise,
Beneath the canvas of soft skies.

In shadows deep, our dreams take flight,
Cloaked in the magic of the night.
Each flame a hope, a story spun,
In forest realms, forever run.

The twilight fades, but we hold fast,
To moments cherished, memories cast.
With every flame, the verdant sings,
In twilight's cradle, life takes wings.

So gather near the fire's glow,
Embrace the warmth, let spirits flow.
For in this night, as shadows wane,
Verdant flames ignite love's refrain.

Whispers of Resilience

In shadows deep, a quiet strength,
Tales of courage span the length.
Through trials faced, we rise anew,
With hearts ablaze, we'll see it through.

Each whispered hope, a guiding light,
Illuminates the darkest night.
Together bound in love's embrace,
We'll forge ahead, no need for haste.

With every storm, a lesson learned,
In flames of struggle, our spirits burned.
Yet like the dawn, we break the chains,
Emerging whole, through joys and pains.

So heed the call, let voices swell,
In unity, we weave our spell.
For in our hearts, the magic lies,
A tapestry where courage flies.

Together, fierce, we stand and rise,
Our laughter ringing 'neath the skies.
In whispers soft, the truth revealed,\nWith resilience deep,
our fates are sealed.

Embered Leaves in the Dawn

Beneath the boughs where daybreak gleams,
Embered leaves dance in golden dreams.
Their hues ignite the morning air,
With whispered tales of joy and care.

A fragile peace upon the ground,
As nature stirs with gentle sound.
The sun awakes, its fingers play,
On every branch, in bright array.

Each droplet glimmers, fresh with light,
Awakening the spirits bright.
Through every leaf, a story told,
Of silent strength and hearts of gold.

The dawn, a promise, fair and true,
Where hope unfurls, and dreams renew.
In every rustle, life takes flight,
Guided by the dawn's soft light.

So cherish now, this fleeting hour,
When nature blooms in quiet power.
Held in the arms of morn's embrace,
We find our peace in nature's grace.

The Flame Beneath the Fronds

Nestled low where shadows play,
A glimmer caught, a fire's sway.
The fronds above, they softly sigh,
Guarding secrets, reaching high.

Within the earth, where roots entwine,
A silent strength begins to shine.
Though seen by few, it burns so bright,
A beacon fierce in darkest night.

Each flicker sparks a distant dream,
A unity, a warming beam.
Relentless, like the wildest storm,
The pulse of life begins to warm.

So tread with care beneath these trees,
Where whispered winds share ancient keys.
For every flame, a tale of yore,
Can ignite the hearts, forevermore.

In every frond, a tale concealed,\nThe unyielding flame
shall be revealed.
With courage fierce beneath the fronds,
Awake, arise, and forge beyond.

Verdant Fireflies in the Gloom

In twilight's hush, the fireflies gleam,
Like scattered sparks upon a dream.
They dance through shadows, bright and bold,
Their stories whispered, softly told.

With every flicker, hope ignites,
Illuminating starry nights.
In darkest hours, they flutter free,
Reminding us of what can be.

Beneath the stars, their magic flares,
A symphony that whispers prayers.
In leaps of light, they break the gloom,
Creating paths through night's dark womb.

So let them guide your weary heart,
As among the trees, their lights depart.
For in the dim, they herald grace,
A tapestry in nature's space.

Embrace the glow, let spirits rise,
As fireflies weave across the skies.
In verdant meadows, dreams take wing,
With every breath, new hope they bring.

Embers of Verdant Dreams

In twilight's shroud, where whispers dwell,
The nature sings a silent spell.
Beneath the leaves, the secrets lie,
As fireflies dance in the dusky sky.

Among the roots where shadows creep,
The earth holds wonders, buried deep.
With every pulse, the green heart beats,
In harmony where magic meets.

Through tangled vines of emerald hue,
Fortunes bloom, with morning dew.
The visions spark in fertile minds,
As dreams arise, and hope unwinds.

Awake, oh spirits, heed the call,
For nature's song enfolds us all.
In every petal, every beam,
Are living tales of verdant dreams.

With each new dawn, the world ignites,
A canvas painted with endless sights.
To rise above, let courage seem,
For life is born from verdant dreams.

Whispering Green Flames

In secret glades where shadows play,
The whispers kiss the break of day.
A rustling breeze, like ancient tales,
Awakens life where hope prevails.

Emerald fingers reach for light,
As sparks of joy take wing in flight.
Through tangled branches, stories weave,
In every breath, the forest leaves.

The gentle sway of grasses green,
Holds memories of what has been.
With every flicker, life takes form,
In nature's hearth, the spirit's warm.

With every glance, the heart can feel,
The pulse of life in the familiar kneel.
A world reborn, where magic frames,
The tapestry of whispering flames.

In the rich soil, the futures thrive,
The arching trees, forever alive.
So listen close, and let hope reclaim,
The song of souls in green flames.

Revival Through the Lush Canopy

Where sunlight births the morning dew,
The canopy cloaks the vibrant hue.
Each leaf unfurls, a story old,
Of journeys past in emerald gold.

Through branches high, the light will dance,
In shadowed glades, the spirits prance.
A symphony of life awakes,
Through ancient woods, the heartbeat shakes.

The river's song, a soothing balm,
Unravels senses, thick and calm.
A forest deep, where wild thoughts roam,
Find solace here, and feel at home.

In nature's arms, anew we rise,
With every breeze that graces skies.
The world revives, through lush embrace,
A sanctuary, a sacred space.

So let your spirit wander wide,
Amidst the trees where secrets hide.
Through this revival, feel the sway,
Of nature's grace, and find your way.

Igniting Nature's Kindling

In hidden glens where spirits breathe,
Nature stirs, her gifts to bequeath.
With tender care, she fans the fire,
Of life reborn, with pure desire.

From ashes rise the seeds of fate,
In every bloom, a pathway gate.
The dance of petals, soft and bright,
Ignites the heart, a warm delight.

Through woodland paths where shadows blend,
Each step we take, the earth extends.
To whisper secrets from within,
As kindling burns, our souls begin.

With every spark, a tale unfolds,
Of timeless truths and dreams untold.
So seek the flame in nature's heart,
For light awaits to guide our start.

Awake, dear souls, to life anew,
Let all your passions come into view.
In joyous hearts, find love's pure thread,
Igniting nature's kindling ahead.

Verdant Whispers of Radiance

In emerald depths, the secrets hide,
Where sunlight pours, and murmurs glide.
The leaves converse in hushed delight,
Awakening dreams in the fading light.

Soft breezes carry tales of old,
Of magic spun and wonders told.
Each blade of grass, a story's end,
In nature's book, forever penned.

The flowers nod in vibrant cheer,
Reminders of what we hold dear.
With every bloom, a promise new,
As whispers weave the morning dew.

A tapestry in hues so bright,
Each shadow cast, a dance of light.
Verdant whispers call the heart,
And in their chorus, we impart.

So pause a while, let magic soar,
In every breath, the earth's rapport.
Embrace the sounds, the sights, the grace,
In verdant realms, find your place.

The Flame's Dance in the Green

Among the ferns, a flicker gleams,
A fire ignites beneath the beams.
With every sway, the shadows play,
In harmony with night and day.

The leaves are charmed by ember's glow,
As stars lean low to watch the show.
In nature's arms, the flames do twirl,
A glowing heart in twilight's whirl.

Through branches thick, the sparks ascend,
In wild abandon, they descend.
The whispering winds lend soft embrace,
As dances weave a timeless space.

With each new flicker, life awakes,
In vibrant hues, the stillness shakes.
A bright effulgence, fierce yet kind,
In every heartbeat, warmth we find.

So let the flame and forest blend,
A dance of life without an end.
In every shimmer, give a chance,
To feel the pulse of nature's dance.

Nature's Relation of Light and Life

In dawn's embrace, the world ignites,
A canvas painted with pure delights.
The golden rays caress the trees,
In harmony with the gentle breeze.

The river sings a silver song,
Where shadows dwell, and echoes throng.
Each ripple holds a tale to tell,
Of laughter shared in nature's swell.

The mountains rise with prideful grace,
Reflecting light in a silent space.
A bond of earth, of sky, of air,
In unity, they breathe and care.

As twilight falls, the stars appear,
In cosmic dance, the night draws near.
Each twinkling light a guiding voice,
That whispers softly, "Rejoice, rejoice."

Thus, nature weaves her thread of life,
A tapestry of joy and strife.
In every moment, light ignites,
A testament in day and nights.

Lively Emotions in the Canopy

Beneath the boughs, where dreams reside,
The canopy blooms, a world inside.
With vibrant colors, hearts align,
In every shade, a tale divine.

The laughter pauses, shadows tease,
As sunlight filters through the leaves.
Each rustling branch, a cavalcade,
Of lively whispers, unafraid.

In every branch, a heartbeat shared,
A symphony of souls declared.
The dance of creatures, swift and free,
In nature's arms, we long to be.

With every flicker, joy awakes,
In vibrant hues, the spirit shakes.
A canvas brightens with each hue,
Emotions painted, ever true.

So linger here, in lush embrace,
Where lively moments find their place.
In dappled light, let sorrows flee,
And celebrate the canopy.

The Glimmering Heart of the Grove

In the heart of the ancient wood,
Where whispers of magic softly stood,
A glimmer danced on emerald leaves,
Cradling secrets that nature weaves.

Sunlight filters through tangled vines,
As laughter sings in silver lines,
Creatures gather, all aglow,
In the magic that the forest knows.

Each step a promise, each pause a song,
In a world where the wild belongs,
The glimmering heart pulses bright,
Illuminating shadows with light.

Beneath the boughs, dreams take flight,
As moonlight bathes the grove in white,
With every breath, a story unfolds,
Of valiant knights and treasures old.

So linger here, in this timeless place,
Where time stands still, in quiet grace,
For the heart of the grove will always beat,
In harmony where the wondrous meet.

Revival in the Shade of Flames

In the shadows where embers glow,
Life finds a way, despite the woe,
Through flickering light and whispered fears,
A revival stirs amidst the tears.

The flames that once brought forth despair,
Now dance as spirits fill the air,
A phoenix rises, strong and free,
In the ash, a new destiny.

Amidst the heat, new blooms appear,
Emboldened whispers, bright and clear,
Each petal brushed by fiery touch,
A lesson learned, and oh, so much.

In the depths of darkest night,
Hope returns, a guiding light,
With courage gathered from the pain,
We find our strength to rise again.

So let the embers guide our way,
As we embrace the dawning day,
For even in the fiercest fight,
Revival blooms, a pure delight.

Blazing Trails of Leafy Glory

Through winding paths of leafy grace,
A riot of colors, nature's embrace,
Joy spills forth in vibrant hues,
Upon the trails we dare to choose.

With every step on forest's floor,
Stories echo, tales of yore,
Of whispered dreams and laughter bright,
In a tapestry woven by shimmering light.

Branches reach with eager hands,
Holding wonders of this land,
The songs of birds a sweet refrain,
In the heart of glory, none in vain.

As twilight weaves its silken thread,
And stars awaken overhead,
The blazing trails will never fade,
In the dance of joy, we are remade.

So wander forth, brave hearts and bold,
In leafy glory, let tales unfold,
For in the trails of nature's art,
We find the fire that warms the heart.

Sprouting Amidst a Fiery Quagmire

In a world where shadows loom,
And fiery tempests threaten doom,
Life dares to push through charred remains,
In the quagmire, it breaks the chains.

With roots that brave the heat and strife,
Emerging from the flames of life,
A sprout stands tall, defying fate,
In resilience, we celebrate.

The fiery breath that sought to mar,
Nourishes growth, a guiding star,
For from the fire, new strength is drawn,
A testament to the coming dawn.

Each leaf unfurls with stories told,
Of battles fought, of hearts so bold,
In the quagmire, a courage fierce,
From fiery trials, our souls it pierce.

So let us rise, like seedlings brave,
In the ashes, we learn to save,
For life, amidst turmoil, will find a way,
Through sprouting dreams that light the day.

The Spark of Renewal Beneath the Shade

In whispered woods where shadows play,
The light seeps through in soft ballet.
Each leaf, a tale of battles won,
A spark of hope, a new begun.

Beneath the boughs, where secrets weave,
The heart finds solace, learns to believe.
Roots entwined in ancient grace,
Awake again, this hallowed space.

With gentle breaths, the air anew,
A promise made, a trust held true.
For every ending sparks a flame,
Reviving life, renewing name.

In silence deep, the echoes wake,
Where dreams unspool, and fears forsake.
The dance of dawn in colors bright,
Bestows the world with softest light.

Lush Resilience in Flame's Afterglow

When fiery trials leave their mark,
From ashes cold, a song can spark.
The earth, in pain, begins to heal,
Lush resilience in each revealed.

Amidst the ruins, green shoots rise,
A testament 'neath open skies.
With every hope, they stretch and grow,
In vibrant hues of flame's afterglow.

The sun returns with warming grace,
To bathe the land, embrace its face.
From charred remains, the tendrils crawl,
A tale of strength amidst the fall.

Each breath of wind holds whispered dreams,
In every heart, the courage beams.
From struggle born, we find our way,
In nature's arms, forever sway.

Glistening Grove of Rediscovery

In glistening groves where echoes dwell,
The paths diverge, each tale to tell.
Where memories linger in the air,
A place of dreams, and gentle care.

With every step, the past unfolds,
In dappled light, a journey bold.
The whispering leaves invite the heart,
To seek the truths that lie apart.

A symphony of rustling sound,
Each note a treasure to be found.
In quiet corners, secrets gleam,
In this enchanted, timeless dream.

So take a breath, let worries cease,
In nature's calm, embrace the peace.
For in this grove, we pause and see,
The beauty born of harmony.

The Brightness Beneath the Boughs

Beneath the boughs where shadows play,
The brightness whispers through the fray.
With open hearts and hands aligned,
We weave the light our souls designed.

In every nook, a glimmer shines,
A tapestry of fate combines.
The sunlight spills on emerald ground,
In every pulse, the magic found.

A journey starts with steps of grace,
Guided by stars in quiet space.
With every glance, a spark ignites,
Transforming dreams to soaring heights.

And in the stillness, truths reveal,
The strength within our hearts to heal.
For in the shadow's gentle sway,
The brightness breathes, and hearts obey.

Nature's Incandescent Revival

In the heart of the forest, life stirs anew,
Petals unfold, drenched in morning dew.
Whispers of growth in the soft sunlight,
Colors awaken, banishing the night.

Birds weave songs in the tall, swaying trees,
A melody carried by the gentle breeze.
Nature's canvas, painted bright and wide,
Harmony pulses, a joyous tide.

Streams dance with laughter, a silver thread,
Over smooth stones, where the wild things tread.
Life calls to life in this wondrous tale,
Each pulse of the earth, a mystical trail.

Underneath the soil, secrets unfurl,
Roots intertwining, a hidden whirl.
Every green shoot emerges with grace,
A testament to time's warm embrace.

As shadows lengthen, colors softly fade,
The day's gentle glow, in dusky shade.
Yet hope blooms anew with the morning light,
Nature's revival, a wondrous sight.

Resplendence Among the Shadows

In twilight's embrace, the stars gleam bright,
Casting soft whispers into the night.
Among the shadows, a shimmer unfolds,
Secrets and stories of ages untold.

Moonlight weaves silver through branches above,
Crickets in chorus, a serenade of love.
Each rustle and sigh, a dance of the veils,
Filling the dark with enchanted tales.

Beneath the soft cloak of night's tender care,
Dreams take to flight in the cool evening air.
With each gentle breeze, hope stirs in the heart,
Resplendent whispers, a mystical art.

The fireflies wink in the depth of the woods,
Flickering lights like thoughts in the broods.
They twirl through the air, a bright, fleeting spark,
Illuminating paths through the inky dark.

In shadows, there lives a flicker of grace,
A beauty that hides in still, secret places.
For even in darkness, we find a soft glow,
Resplendence lingers, though few dare to know.

The Emerald Ember's Lament

In the depths of the woods, an ember glows,
A heart once bright, now whispers of woes.
Leaves that once danced in the sun's warm embrace,
Now sigh in the silence, a haunting grace.

Emerald hues fade, lost in the past,
Stories forgotten, shadows are cast.
The flicker of dreams, like the mist in the air,
Lingers in echoes, a lingering dare.

Time's cruel hand shapes the landscape anew,
The vibrant embers dulled by the view.
Yet each fading leaf tells a tale of its own,
Every parting breath a seed to be sown.

Under the canopy, where the wild things roam,
Life pulses gently, finding its home.
Within every sigh, a promise remains,
To rise from the ashes, to break every chain.

The ember may dim, but it never will die,
For in every ending, new beginnings lie.
With roots intertwined, it finds strength to stand,
An emerald lament, a fate woven grand.

Glowing Roots of Resilience

Deep in the earth, where the shadows reside,
Glowing roots stretch forth, with nowhere to hide.
Through soil and stone, they delve and they weave,
Drawing strength from the past, in hopes to believe.

With whispers of winds, and tears from the rain,
They flourish through struggles, endure all our pain.
Each bond and connection, like threads of a seam,
Knits life with a purpose, supports every dream.

In gardens of color, they twine in delight,
Offering warmth and solace, igniting the night.
For nature's soft heartbeat pulses through time,
Resilience glows bright in each leaf and each rhyme.

Beneath every surface, the dance goes on strong,
Whispered in tales ancient, echoed in song.
From the roots to the sky, they grow hand in hand,
Through trials and triumphs, together they stand.

In silence, they carry the weight of the years,
Transforming the pain into laughter and tears.
A tapestry woven, entwined with our fates,
Glowing roots of resilience, love never waits.

The Light Within the Lush

In the heart of the verdant glade,
Where whispers of magic softly fade,
A glow breaks through the emerald leaves,
Nature's dreams, the soul receives.

Beneath the boughs, secrets intertwine,
Each ray of sun, a silver line,
In shadows deep, the spirits play,
Guiding the lost, lighting the way.

Moss blankets stones, a gentle touch,
Reminds us of love that means so much,
In every twinkle, hope resides,
A beacon where the heart abides.

With each dawn, the forest sings,
Of forgotten tales and ancient things,
A symphony of life so pure,
In this embrace, we find our cure.

Through verdant paths, we wander free,
Discovering what we're meant to be,
In the light that filters through the lush,
Our souls awaken, rise from hush.

Ferns of Fire and Memory

In the twilight's soft embrace,
Ferns unfold with tender grace,
Their fronds aglow in evening's fire,
Whispering secrets of desire.

Once in shadows dreams did dwell,
In whispered winds, their stories swell,
Memories dance on the breeze's tongue,
With every heartbeat, they are spun.

Crimson hues and golden trails,
Draw us into their ancient tales,
Each leaf a chapter, bold and bright,
Crafting our world in flickering light.

As embers fade, the night draws near,
Yet the ferns in silence hear,
The echoes of lives long since past,
In realms where love forever lasts.

These emerald coils, through time they weave,
A tapestry of those who believe,
In the fire of heart, the warmth of kin,
In each sharp breath, a world begins.

Echoes of Growth in the Ashes

From the ashes of what once was,
Life emerges, a tireless buzz,
The ground, a cradle for dreams reborn,
In the quietude of the forlorn.

Echoes play on windswept trails,
Stories of hope, where courage prevails,
In the cracks of stone, green shoots sprout,
Nature's whispers, daring to shout.

Through the remnants of yesterday's fight,
New blooms blossom in soft twilight,
Weaving a tale of loss and grace,
In every corner, a sacred space.

With patience drawn from fading light,
Change transforms the dark to bright,
In every heart, the fire glows,
Fostering life in the thorny throes.

Resilience thrives beneath the clay,
In every struggle, come what may,
Ashes bear witness to what we've grown,
In the cycle of life, we're never alone.

Dancing Flames in the Canopy

In the canopy's swaying embrace,
Flames of fire begin their chase,
Flickering light through branches weaves,
A dance of shadows, where magic breathes.

As sunset spills its molten gold,
Secrets of old, the forest told,
In this rhythm, the heart takes flight,
Boundless dreams under the night.

Every flicker tells a tale,
Of spirits daring to prevail,
Within the dance, a story blooms,
In the wild where adventure looms.

As stars peep through the silken leaves,
The dance of flames, the heart believes,
Each spark a wish that roams the skies,
In the magic night, where the soul flies.

So let us join this fervent trance,
With open hearts, we take the chance,
To move in tune with nature's song,
In the dance of life, we all belong.

Flickers Beneath the Shadowed Leaves

In the twilight's soft embrace,
Whispers dance on gentle breeze,
Flickers trace a timeworn path,
Underneath the shadowed trees.

Moonlight weaves a silver thread,
Casting dreams on emerald ground,
Each flicker tells a tale of hope,
In the silence, magic found.

Crickets sing their evening song,
Symphony of night unfolds,
Beneath the canopy so vast,
Secrets of the forest told.

Stars above in velvet sky,
Twinkle like the dreams we hold,
In the stillness, hearts can fly,
Flickers bold, through shadows bold.

Nature's heart, a fleeting glimpse,
In shadows deep, the light shall weave,
Flickers dance, and spirits rise,
Beneath the shadowed, whispered leaves.

Luminary of the Sylvan Spirit

In the heart of ancient wood,
Where the whispers softly tread,
A luminary glides through dusk,
Lighting paths where dreams are led.

With a grace that stirs the night,
Shimmering with a gentle glow,
The spirit guides lost souls afar,
In the depths where wildflowers grow.

Mossy stones and gnarled roots,
All await her shining flight,
While shadows dance in delight,
Chasing tales in silver light.

Through the thicket, shadows weave,
A promise whispered in the air,
The luminary weaves her lore,
In the forest's tender care.

As twilight fades, and stars ignite,
The sylvan spirit journeys near,
With every heartbeat, tales take flight,
In kindred magic, love draws near.

Ferns in a Cascade of Light

Amidst the ferns, a story waits,
In dappled light where shadows play,
Emerald leaves in harmony,
Chasing dreams of night and day.

Beneath the cover of the trees,
A river's song begins to hum,
Ferns sway gently, whisper soft,
As nature's heartbeat starts to strum.

Fluttering wings and rustling leaves,
A dance within the filtered sun,
Life awakens, softly spins,
In the cascade, magic won.

Wrapped in silence, time stands still,
Every glimmer holds a spark,
Ferns in light, a tender grace,
Hearts ignited in the dark.

In this glen, enchantment thrives,
As whispers echo through the night,
Ferns embrace the dreams we seek,
In a cascade, pure and bright.

Blooming After Ashes

From the depths of sorrow's grip,
A seedling breaks the hardened ground,
With every tear that kissed the earth,
Blooming after ashes found.

Where shadows lingered, hope now stirs,
In colors bright, it dares to rise,
A testament to strength within,
Against the canvas of the skies.

Petals open to the sun,
Each hue a story, fiercely spun,
In every bloom, a soul reborn,
Shining bright like morning's run.

The past may whisper of the pain,
But joy can weave through heart's despair,
In blooming leaves, a fragrant promise,
Love arises from the air.

So let the ashes guide your way,
For every ending holds a chance,
To bloom anew, and dance with light,
In life's enchanting, wondrous dance.

A Forest of Flickering Luminescence

In the heart where shadows sway,
A glow ignites the darkened way.
Winking stars of green and gold,
Whisper secrets, tales untold.

Leaves dance gently on the breeze,
Painting dreams among the trees.
Silvery streams of moonlit grace,
Lead the weary to a place.

Where flowers bloom in colors bright,
Casting spells in soft twilight.
Each petal shines, a work of art,
Igniting wonder in the heart.

Creatures flit where shadows blend,
On paths where night and magic tend.
Curious eyes watch from afar,
Charmed beneath the evening star.

A symphony of light and sound,
In this haven, peace is found.
Forever etched in memory's grasp,
The forest's love, an endless clasp.

The Warmth Beneath the Boughs

Beneath the branches, shadows play,
Where sunlight kisses through the gray.
A blanket made of earth and leaves,
Wraps the heart as nature weaves.

The soothing rustle sings of cheer,
A warm embrace, a refuge here.
Through tangled roots and twining vines,
A story whispered, love defines.

In hidden nooks, where spirits rest,
Fables linger, secrets blessed.
A world awaits, where dreams ignite,
And stars spark hope in gentle night.

Time pauses here, as moments blend,
In nature's arms, it seems to mend.
With every sigh, a promise swells,
The warmth beneath, where magic dwells.

Together, hearts in nature tune,
Beneath the vast, embracing moon.
In this embrace, we find our song,
The warmth beneath, where we belong.

Resurgence of the Verdant Light

Awakening from winter's sigh,
The emerald greens begin to rise.
From slumber deep, the earth rebirths,
A vibrant pulse beneath the dirth.

Each blade of grass, a soldier tall,
Defying frost, refusing fall.
Blossoms bloom, their colors bright,
Painting fields in pure delight.

The teeming life stirs in the glade,
Emerald hues, a grand parade.
The sun returns, with kisses sweet,
A warming touch that stirs the street.

Bees dance joyfully in the air,
Echoes of life everywhere.
In every nook, in every cranny,
Hope abides, enchanting many.

Resurgence bright, a joyful song,
All life knows, it can't be wrong.
From roots to blooms, a tale unfolds,
Nature's magic, rich and bold.

Eruptions of Green in the Abyss

In depths where shadows weave and twist,
Eruptions of life that can't be missed.
Emerald bursts from earth's embrace,
Defying silence, claiming space.

Ferns unfurl in the dimmest light,
Transforming darkness, sheer delight.
Moss blankets stones, a velvet spread,
Whispering tales of all that's dead.

In crevices, wildflowers sprout,
Coloring corners once in doubt.
Petals brave in vivid hue,
Painting hope where none once grew.

Even in gloom, life finds a way,
A dance of green that dares to play.
Roots entwined, a bond so deep,
In the abyss, dreams softly creep.

Echoes of laughter, secrets tease,
In every rustle of the leaves.
These eruptions show a truth profound,
In darkness' clutch, life can abound.

Luminous Flora's Resilient Rise

In shadows deep, the flowers bloom,
A dance of light dispels the gloom.
Through trials faced, they find their way,
Emerging strong with each new day.

Roots entwined in earth so grand,
They stretch their arms, a vibrant band.
With colors bold, they paint the skies,
A testament to nature's ties.

From whispered winds and gentle rains,
The beauty flourishes, never wanes.
Each petal sings a tale of might,
In every dawn, they claim the light.

Beneath the stars, their secrets weave,
A tapestry that none believe.
Through darkest nights, they hold their ground,
In resilience, true strength is found.

So let us pause and heed the charm,
Of flora's grace, of nature's balm.
For in their rise, a lesson clear,
In every heart, we conquer fear.

Ferns' Bright Dances in the Ashes

In the heart of ruins, green unfolds,
Ferns stretch out, their stories told.
From ashes cold, their spirits rise,
A verdant echo, shrouded skies.

They sway and twirl in silent glee,
A soft embrace, wild and free.
In shadows cast, they find their place,
In every nook, a gentle grace.

With fronds that whisper ancient lore,
They greet the sun, forevermore.
In winding paths, their courage shows,
Through tangled fate, pure beauty grows.

In fires past, they've found their song,
With vibrant steps, they dance along.
Through time's embrace, they bear the mark,
Of survival bright within the dark.

So let us learn from nature's art,
To rise anew, to make a start.
Like ferns that flourish where all seems lost,
We find our way, despite the cost.

Shimmering Life Beneath the Canopy

In tangled branches overhead,
A world of whispers, life is fed.
Beneath the boughs, a hidden dance,
Where creatures play and shadows prance.

The softest sighs of gentle streams,
Awaken dreams in tender beams.
With every rustle, secrets shared,
In leaves that flutter, love declared.

A vibrant hum of life's refrain,
In the hush of leaves, joy remains.
From critters small to soaring flight,
The canopy holds magic's light.

In dappled sun, the moments gleam,
A tapestry spun from nature's dream.
Each heartbeat thrums in harmony,
Beneath the vast, embracing tree.

So wander deep where wild things roam,
In nature's arms, we find our home.
For in each glimmer, life's embrace,
Awaits us there, a sacred space.

Fireflies in a Sea of Green

In twilight's glow, they flicker bright,
Dancing stars in the depth of night.
With fleeting sparks, they light the way,
Through fields of green, where shadows play.

A gentle breeze, their partners sway,
In joyous flight, they find their way.
As if the sky had spilled its dreams,
In every glow, a wish redeems.

In secret glades and whispered trails,
Their magic sparkles, never pales.
A symphony of flickering cheer,
Each tiny light brings wonders near.

So pause and gaze, let heart take wing,
As fireflies weave their soothing string.
In nature's dance, we find our peace,
In every light, our spirits cease.

For in these moments, time stands still,
As night unfolds with grace and thrill.
Though fleeting be their vibrant gleam,
They linger long within our dream.

Fractal Flames of a New Era

In patterns bright, the flames dance bright,
They flicker bold, then fade from sight.
Each spiral bold, a tale untold,
In fractal echoes, futures unfold.

With every spark, a choice ignites,
In shadows cast, the heart takes flight.
Reflections swell, in hues of gold,
A symphony vast, where life is bold.

Around the fire, the whispers call,
Of dreams reborn, as embers fall.
An era wakes, with voices clear,
In fractal flames, we conquer fear.

The skies alight, with colors rare,
A tapestry woven, with utmost care.
The future calls, and hearts entwine,
In this new dawn, our hopes align.

So gather close, beneath the stars,
In warmth of flame, we heal our scars.
Through fractal paths, we find our way,
To brighter realms, where we shall stay.

Rebirth in the Canopy's Embrace

Beneath the leaves, where shadows play,
Life stirs anew, at break of day.
In gentle greens, the whispers sing,
A song of earth, of every spring.

With sunlight's touch, old wounds are healed,
In roots entwined, our fate revealed.
From bark and bud, fresh hopes arise,
A world reborn, beneath the skies.

The canopy holds secrets tight,
In every creak, a whispered plight.
Yet in the dark, new blooms ignite,
A promise made, to brave the night.

With every breeze, there's life, anew,
The dance of leaves, shades of all hue.
In nature's arms, we find our place,
In canopy's embrace, we find grace.

So cherish roots that hold us strong,
In every branch, we all belong.
Among the trees, our spirits soar,
In rebirth's grace, forevermore.

Fleeting Glimmers of Florals

In gardens blooming, color bright,
A dance of petals, pure delight.
With morning dew, they greet the sun,
Each gentle bud, a race begun.

Fleeting glimmers, a moment rare,
A soft perfume fills the air.
In every hue, a story shares,
Of love once lost, and hopes and cares.

They blossom forth, then fade away,
Yet still they leave their sweet bouquet.
In every heart, their beauty grows,
A memory held in nature's throes.

Through seasons' change, they teach us well,
That life is brief, like a whisper's shell.
Yet in their grace, we find our way,
In fleeting glimmers, bright and gay.

So plant the seeds of love and light,
In every heart, let dreams take flight.
For in the garden's tender care,
Fleeting glimmers linger there.

The Aglow Between the Shadows

In twilight's grip, the world holds breath,
A whisper soft, of life and death.
Between the dark, a light shall grow,
In embers of hope, a subtle glow.

The shadows dance, a restless sway,
In hidden corners, dreams won't stray.
A glimmer sparked, in hearts aglow,
From ancient tales, where wisdom flows.

With every step, the path is trod,
In stillness found, we glimpse the odd.
Through curtain night, a promise calls,
A guiding star, that never falls.

So fear not dusk; it brings the dawn,
For in the night, we are reborn.
The aglow holds, both peace and strife,
In shadows cast, we find our life.

Embrace the dark, for light will rise,
In every heart, the sun shall prize.
Through both the light and shadows cast,
We journey forth, our spirits vast.

Radiance in the Understory

Beneath the boughs where shadows play,
Soft whispers call at break of day.
The sunlight filters, warm and bright,
In every leaf, a spark of light.

With dew-kissed petals, blooms emerge,
In silence, dreams and thoughts converge.
The pulse of life begins anew,
In hidden parts, the wild breaks through.

A tapestry of green and gold,
Tales of magic softly told.
Each creature small, each sound profound,
In quiet grace, the world surrounds.

The understory, rich and deep,
Holds secrets that the ancients keep.
In every rustle, truth is found,
A symphony of vibrant sound.

So venture forth, let spirits rise,
In nature's midst, where wonder lies.
Take heart in whispers of the trees,
And flow with life, like gentle breeze.

Nature's Quiet Rebirth

In winter's grasp, the world lies still,
Yet deep below, the earth does thrill.
The seeds lie curled in dreams' embrace,
Awaiting warmth to spark their race.

With gentle rains and warming sun,
Soft whispers tell the time has come.
A crocus peeks from snowy rest,
The herald of spring's tender quest.

The robin sings, the brook awakes,
New life emerges with every shake.
In vibrant hues, the wildflowers bloom,
Chasing away the winter's gloom.

The trees don cloaks of fresh, new leaves,
Their branches dance as nature weaves.
Each note of life, a song reborn,
As day breaks forth and greets the morn.

With every heartbeat, life unfolds,
Nature's beauty, a tale retold.
In quiet moments, peace is found,
As earth spins softly round and round.

Ashen Roots

In haunted woods where shadows creep,
The remnants of a fire weep.
Charred branches whisper tales of old,
Of dreams once bright, now grey and cold.

Amidst the ash, a glimmer shines,
In fractured earth, hope intertwines.
From ashen roots, the brave will rise,
Towards the light, beyond the skies.

The forest grieves yet yearns to mend,
For every beginning finds its end.
Life dances close to death's dark seam,
In every crack, a tender dream.

New ferns unfurl, in green they cloak,
The scars that linger, like a joke.
Yet from despair, a beauty flows,
With every wound, the wild still grows.

So take the path where shadows lie,
Discover truth as embers die.
In silence, find what time can teach,
For every heart can learn to reach.

Verdant Dreams

In emerald depths where secrets sleep,
The dreams of nature softly creep.
With every breeze, a breath of life,
Where time flows gently, free from strife.

Beneath the trees, the earth is warm,
A sanctuary, safe from harm.
Where creatures dance and rivers flow,
In verdant realms, the magic grows.

The sunlight filters through the leaves,
In dappled light, the heart believes.
A symphony of chirps and sighs,
In leafy nooks, the spirit flies.

With every shade, a story traced,
In whispered winds, dreams interlaced.
Through tangled vines, adventure calls,
In nature's breath, the wonder sprawls.

So wander forth, embrace the green,
In every moment, life is seen.
To dwell in dreams, both wild and free,
In nature's arms, find destiny.

Glimmers in the Shaded Grove

In twilight hours, the forest glows,
With soft-lit paths where mystery flows.
A flicker here, a shimmer there,
In secret places, magic's flare.

Mossy beds and dim-lit trails,
Where whispers echo, truth prevails.
The softest touch of cool night air,
Invites the stars to dance and share.

Among the roots, old stories weave,
In shadows cast, we dare believe.
The dance of fireflies, a living spell,
In the shaded grove, all hearts rebel.

With every step, the wild unfolds,
A tapestry of dreams retold.
In nature's law, our spirits find,
The glimmers bright, forever kind.

So linger here, let wonder grow,
In every breath, let magic flow.
With open heart, and curious mind,
In shaded grove, true peace you'll find.

The Warmth of Green Rejuvenation

In the cradle of spring's gentle hand,
New leaves unfurl where the shadows stand.
Whispers of life in the soft, warm breeze,
Nature awakes with grace and ease.

Buds blossom bright, a colorful dance,
Under the sun, every stem finds its chance.
The earth dons a cloak of emerald hue,
A symphony played by the morning dew.

Streams of laughter in the garden's heart,
Each petal a canvas, a delicate art.
The warmth of the season wraps tight like a shawl,
A promise of magic, renewing us all.

In the quiet corners, secrets unfold,
Whispers of stories from ages of old.
Life intertwines in a tapestry bright,
Under moonlit watch, throughout the night.

As twilight deepens, shadows will play,
Guiding the dreamers who wander and sway.
In the warmth of green, we find our retreat,
With every heartbeat, our spirits complete.

Embrace of Fire and Flourish

In the hearth of night, embers appear,
Dancing like spirits, bright without fear.
A crackling warmth, it pulls us near,
In the glow of fire, our path's made clear.

Flames leap and twirl, in a fiery waltz,
Igniting the sky with vibrant vaults.
Each flicker a promise, each spark a dream,
In its embrace, all worries seem.

Colors of amber paint shadows long,
With echoes of laughter, the night feels strong.
The firelight whispers, tales of the past,
Binding us closer, together at last.

Among the flames, our fears uncoil,
In the sacred circle, we share our toil.
For in this embrace, we flourish and rise,
A dance of connection beneath the skies.

As dawn approaches, the embers fade,
Yet in our hearts, the warmth is laid.
Forever ignited, our spirits entwined,
In the embrace of fire, true peace we find.

Luminous Spirits of the Forest

In the whispering woods where the shadows play,
Luminous spirits guide the way.
Glowing like lanterns, they weave through the trees,
Unraveling mysteries on the evening breeze.

Underneath stars that twinkle and gleam,
Dreamers gather, wrapped in a dream.
With every rustle and each gentle sigh,
The secrets of woodlands lift softly to fly.

Spirits of laughter float free in the night,
Chasing away darkness, embracing the light.
Connection with nature, so deep and profound,
In the heart of the forest, true magic is found.

Each path we wander reveals hidden bliss,
In the glow of the spirits, we find our kiss.
Moments like fireflies, fleeting yet bright,
A tapestry woven, in shadows and light.

As dawn's first light paints the world anew,
We'll carry the magic, in everything we do.
For the luminous spirits of forest and glade,
Reside in our hearts, never to fade.

Breaths of Fire Among the Foliage

Through tangled leaves, the firelight weaves,
A story of warmth that the night believes.
With flickering tongues that kiss the night air,
Each heartbeat of ember, a tender prayer.

Among the foliage, a feast of delight,
Where shadows dance softly, lost in the light.
The fragrance of pine and burning wood,
Wraps us in laughter, we're understood.

The crackle and pop of the warming flame,
Calls forth the wild, igniting our name.
With each breath of fire, our spirits align,
In this sacred moment, pure hearts intertwine.

Through rustling branches, life takes a breath,
In the glowing embrace, we conquer death.
The cycle of seasons, ever renewed,
From ashes to embers, old dreams are pursued.

As daylight bids farewell with a sigh,
We gather our stories under the sky.
In the breaths of fire, forever we stand,
Bonded by magic, hand in hand.

A Tapestry of Flame and Fern

In twilight's breath, the shadows dance,
Flames flicker low, a fleeting chance.
Fern fronds whisper ancient lore,
Woven stories forevermore.

Across the vale where secrets lie,
Embers rise to greet the sky.
Nature's quilt, stitched with care,
Emboldened hearts embrace the flare.

Through tangled roots, the fire spreads,
Awakening dreams long left for dead.
A tapestry of life reborn,
With every crackle, hope is worn.

The nightingale sings, a haunting tune,
While ferns in moonlight softly croon.
Together they mark the fleeting hour,
In harmony, they wield their power.

With every flicker a tale unfolds,
Of bravery found and the daring bold.
A tapestry rich, in colors bright,
Flame and fern, a wondrous sight.

Ethereal Lights in the Wilderness

In wild terrains where spirits glow,
Ethereal lights in a moonlit show.
Crickets serenade the night,
As stars twinkle with pure delight.

Deep in the woods where shadows creep,
A hidden world awakens from sleep.
Whispers float on the gentle breeze,
Secrets exchanged among the trees.

Among the ferns, a path reveals,
Soft glimmers tell of timeless seals.
Woven life's stories at every turn,
In nature's heart, we'll forever yearn.

The fireflies dance like fairy kin,
Casting spells of wonder within.
Each flicker, a lantern of dreams,
In wilderness where magic teems.

To wander beneath the starlit veil,
In ethereal lands where wonders prevail.
The woods invite us, hearts open wide,
With every step, true magic resides.

Fern Fables of the Radiant

Beneath the boughs of emerald hue,
Fern fables whisper, ancient and true.
Each frond a tale of love and loss,
In the forest, secrets embossed.

Radiant sunbeams filter through,
Caressing greens as if they knew.
A dance of shadows, a gentle sway,
Nature's stories, come what may.

In whispered winds, you'll hear their plea,
Legends shared as old as the sea.
A journey begun with courage born,
Through ferny realms, the heart is torn.

Each dewdrop glints with radiant grace,
A moment captured in time and space.
Fables spoken in hushed tones,
Echo through ages, like ancient stones.

In the quiet dusk when day meets night,
Fern fables linger, hearts take flight.
With every step on this sacred ground,
In nature's embrace, true peace is found.

Illuminated Growth in Fire's Wake

From ash and ember, new life breaks,
Illuminated growth, the heart awakes.
In the wake of flames, a rebirth song,
Nature's promise, where we belong.

Through charred remains, green tends to bloom,
Transforming despair into sweet perfume.
Hope rises high with the sun's first rays,
In fire's wake, a bright new phase.

Each sprout a testament, brave and true,
To endure the storms, to start anew.
In every fern, a story grows,
Of resilience shown when the fire blows.

Beneath the scars of once blackened earth,
Life finds a way to rekindle mirth.
From darkness rises an emerald tide,
In fire's wake, we can abide.

With every flicker, a chance to learn,
From ashes born, let the spirit burn.
Illuminated paths, with courage laid,
In nature's arms, our fears allayed.

Luminary Leaves of the Undergrowth

In shadows deep where whispers dwell,
The leaves take flight with stories to tell.
Each rustle soft, a gentle breath,
Awakening dreams in the silence of death.

They shimmer bright in dappled light,
A tapestry woven of day and night.
Where faeries dance and shadows play,
The undergrowth hums, come what may.

With hues of emerald and gold they sway,
Underneath the boughs where lost souls stray.
The luminary leaves, a guiding flame,
Calling the restless by name.

In secret glades where magic stirs,
Each leaf breathes life, where the fair folk purrs.
A sanctuary for the hearts that roam,
These timeless woods shall always be home.

So wander deep, let your spirit fly,
Trust in the whispers of the woodland sky.
For in each leaf, a tale unfolds,
Of secrets kept and dreams retold.

Wick of the Woodland's Soul

Beneath the boughs, where shadows twine,
The flicker of light in the heart does shine.
A wick ignites in the hollowed wood,
Binding the magic where once it stood.

Embers whisper in the gloaming air,
Stirring the dreams of those unaware.
The soul of the forest breathes with grace,
In every flicker, a warm embrace.

The twilight forms a gauzy veil,
Where secrets weave, and echoes sail.
From ancient roots to skyward climb,
The wick holds fast through the sands of time.

With every spark, a story lives,
Gifted by life the woodland gives.
The warmth of the hearth guides the lost,
In nature's arms, we count the cost.

So heed the glow, let it unfold,
An invitation to be bold.
For with each step upon this path,
The wick of wonder ignites our wrath.

Nature's Dancing Hearth

In glens adorned with vibrant cheer,
The dance of nature draws us near.
With every step, the rhythm flows,
A hearth of life where the wild wind blows.

The crackling branches weave their song,
Beckoning all, both weak and strong.
Around the flames of leaves aglow,
The woodland's spirit puts on a show.

With twirls and leaps, the flowers sigh,
In colors spun beneath the sky.
Fruitful dreams in the cool night air,
Nature's hearth sings, with love to share.

As stars emerge in velvet skies,
The moonlit beams turn whispers to cries.
Each flicker of light in the dancing shade,
Is magic born from the earth once laid.

So join the dance in the crisp night's fold,
Let your heart be wild, let your spirit unfold.
For in every step, a new tale we write,
At nature's hearth, all is alight.

The Glowing Echo of Greenery

In emerald hues, the forest sighs,
A symphony of life beneath the skies.
Each leaf a note, a timeless song,
The echoes of nature, where all belong.

With every whisper, the branches sway,
In harmony with the light of day.
The glowing echoes dance in tune,
Guiding the dreamers beneath the moon.

Where rivers laugh and shadows play,
The lush green world holds sway.
In every grove, a tale awaits,
Of life and magic behind the gates.

As morning sun breaks through the dark,
The glow unveils the woodland's spark.
In every rustle, a story echoing,
Of ancient paths, of the winds softly blowing.

So pause a while, let the stillness in,
Listen close to the tale within.
For in the glow of the greenery bright,
We find our solace in nature's light.

Fern Fronds and Flickering Hearts

In the glade where shadows dance,
Fern fronds sway in gentle trance.
Flickering sparks, a beacon's light,
Guide lost souls through the fragile night.

Whispers weave through emerald leaves,
Stories held in the heart believes.
With every breath, the forest sighs,
Embracing hopes beneath the skies.

Moonlit paths ring with silence deep,
Secrets offered that nature keeps.
With every turn, old magic stirs,
In every pulse, the wonder purrs.

Beneath the stars, where dreams entwine,
Hearts ignite, like wine and brine.
Bound by roots, in harmony's grace,
Fern fronds bloom, finding their place.

In the tapestry of woods so old,
Flickering hearts in stories told.
May we wander where wild things dwell,
In the whispers, find our spell.

Revival in the Green Shadows

Beyond the veil where echoes fade,
In green shadows, new dreams are laid.
Nature's brush paints life anew,
In tender hues of vibrant dew.

Softly sings the nightingale's tune,
Underneath the watchful moon.
A hint of magic in the air,
Revival whispers, everywhere.

Elder trees stretch towards the skies,
With ancient wisdom in their sighs.
Every petal holds a secret right,
In shadows deep, where hearts take flight.

Through tangled vines, old stories rise,
Beneath the mist, the heart replies.
With every step, we greet the dawn,
In the green shadows, life goes on.

Awake, awake! The world today,
In verdant dreams, we find our way.
The spirit's dance, a lovely show,
Revival blooms in soft, sweet flow.

Echoes of the Phoenix Whisper

In the ashes where hopes once lay,
Echoes of the phoenix sway.
A lullaby of flame and flight,
Whispers promise to ignite the night.

Through the darkness, a flicker bold,
Tales of rebirth begin to unfold.
From the embers, life shall rise,
In the dawn beneath azure skies.

Cinders drift like stars from the past,
Memories linger, forever cast.
The heart knows well, its path is clear,
In the song of the phoenix, loud and near.

Each heartbeat a drum of forgotten lore,
Resilient spirit, forever in store.
Through every trial, light finds a way,
In echoes of whispers, come what may.

So rise, dear soul, with passion unfurled,
Be the fire that rewrites the world.
In the dance of rebirth, take your place,
For the phoenix whispers of love's embrace.

Sparkling Greens in Scorched Earth

In lands where flames once fiercely roared,
Now sparkling greens, life's sweet reward.
From scorched earth, a dream takes flight,
With tender shoots, a wondrous sight.

Beneath the surface, hope lies deep,
Awaiting rains for seeds to reap.
A gentle touch, the earth breathes sighs,
As nature weaves its brilliant ties.

Each leaf unfurling, a tale retold,
In shades of emerald, bright and bold.
Life's dance is woven with every thread,
In every heartbeat, promise spread.

Amidst the ashes, beauty thrives,
Where once were struggles, love now drives.
In sparkling greens, a world reborn,
From scorched earth, new life is sworn.

So let us celebrate the light,
In the wake of darkness, joyous flight.
For every end betrays a birth,
In sparkling greens on scorched earth.